War for Empire in Western Pennsylvania

W9-ARV-401

Produced by the Fort Ligonier
Association, in collaboration with
Bushy Run Battlefield, Fort Necessity
National Battlefield and the Fort
Pitt Museum

This publication is produced by the Fort Ligonier
Association, in collaboration with Bushy Run
Battlefield, Fort Necessity National Battlefield
and the Fort Pitt Museum.

This publication is supported jointly by grants
from the Pennsylvania Historical and Museum
Commission, the National Park Service and the
H. John Heinz III Charitable Trust.

ISBN 0-912627-45-X .

Printed in the United States of America.

Cover Illustration:
**General Johnson Saving a Wounded French
Officer from the Tomahawk of a North American
Indian** *by Benjamin West, circa 1764-1768.*
Derby Museum and Art Gallery

*This composition, painted in England by
Pennsylvania artist Benjamin West (1738-1820),
dramatizes a scene from the war for empire in
North America. Sir William Johnson (center),
the Superintendent of Indian Affairs, is in the act
of protecting an injured French officer from the
wrath of a Native American warrior, an ally of
the British. In the immediate foreground are two
British light infantrymen, probably from the
Forty-fourth Regiment of Foot (left) and the
Sixtieth Regiment of Foot (right), both of which
saw service in western Pennsylvania. Behind them
are the long lines of a battalion of foot, and an
unidentified fort looms in the rear. This work is
symbolic of the three contending parties in the war
for empire in western Pennsylvania: France and
Canada, Great Britain and the Thirteen Colonies,
and Native America.*

"Nature itself has conspired to render the River Ohio hereabouts a place of consequence of all the people of North America that are within reach of it . . . ."
Cartographer John Mitchell, 1755

Part 1

Introduction to the War for Empire

A brick and stone blockhouse, no more than twenty feet on a side, stands at the edge of the grass and fountains that are Point State Park. Elegant and strong in its simplicity, the blockhouse has a stone plaque over its entrance that reads "AD 1764 Coll. Bouquet." Here is the oldest surviving building in all of western Pennsylvania. The nearby skyscrapers, bridges, highways and stadium of Pittsburgh dominate the landscape. Yet these modern phenomena, accompanied by the constant din of traffic, seem to flow into this quiet spot where the mighty Ohio River begins.

Pittsburgh, standing at the confluence of the Monongahela and Allegheny Rivers, has a long and fascinating history. Anyone visiting this beautiful setting, with its wide rivers and high bluffs, will know that it has seen its share of important events. Not so long ago, decaying buildings crowded the point at the Forks of the Ohio. All of those are now gone, and, as the community goes about its busy life, there is a sense in the park of a time past.

Almost two-and-a-half centuries have passed since the frontier came through this mountainous country on its relentless march west. All frontiers tend to have common characteristics. A hostile environment attracts tough and ambitious souls who are dissatisfied and often at odds with life in more settled parts. The risks of moving into a frontier are high, but the rewards for the survivor can be great. The dense forests, steep slopes and swift rivers of the Allegheny Mountains were once the scene of a desperate struggle to settle and exploit a wilderness with evidently inexhaustible riches. For more than a decade, the two strongest European nations dispatched traders, soldiers and, inevitably, settlers into the region. A violent, winner-take-all clash introduced the world to names like Monongahela, Allegheny and Ohio. In this war for empire, both France and Great Britain realized that the ultimate prize was control of an entire continent north and east of the vast Spanish holdings of the western hemisphere.

By 1750, the first permanent English and French colonies in America were a century and a half old, but much of the immense interior was little known to Europeans. French voyagers had paddled their canoes through a seemingly endless chain of lakes and rivers. Their trading posts, forts and Jesuit missions ran thousands of miles from the St. Lawrence River to modern Minnesota and down the Mississippi River to New Orleans. As they erected stockades in the forests and piled up beaver pelts for the long and dangerous passage to Montreal, these *coureurs de bois* (runners of the woods) knew their foothold in New France was fragile. There simply was too much wilderness to yield to the limited supplies and manpower of the French.

"An European...must have lived some time in the vast forest of America; otherwise he will hardly be able to conceive a continuity of woods without end." That is how the Swiss soldier Colonel Henry Bouquet put it, knowing that a forest the size of Europe dictated its own terms to anyone bold enough to enter. In today's world of shrinking resources, it is almost impossible to conceive the awe-inspiring presence of the "Big Woods." To the European colonists and their progeny, this ocean of towering trees was both a fearsome obstacle and redoubtable adversary.

One important player in this drama had learned to live with and to thrive in this environment. The eastern Native American had prospered in a technologically unsophisticated, but adaptable, culture centuries old. These Indians were excellent hunters, and far from being nomads, were probably the best farmers on the continent in the eighteenth century. Contrary to myth, they had established religions and tribal social structures more

The Arms of France.
National Museums of Canada

A remnant of the original forest that once covered western Pennsylvania. The tall, straight trees and dense canopy curtailed the sunlight, stifling undergrowth and giving the forest its characteristically "gloomy" appearance. The sheer vastness and extent of the "woods without end" created a far different look from that of today's forests. This scene was taken in Cook State Forest (Pennsylvania).

productive of harmony than violence. The Woodland Indian lived in permanent communities and created exquisite decorative arts. Native self-confidence was expressed in such tribal names as *Lenni Lenape* (the real people) for the Delaware and *Ongwe Honwe* (the original people) for the Iroquois.

European settlement inexorably brought change that ultimately led to disaster for Native Americans. From the beginning of colonial settlement, the clash of cultures developed into a pattern which kept repeating itself across the continent. In the Ohio Valley traders offered astonishing things; metal tools and weapons, cloth and garments, mirrors and cosmetics. But they also introduced the Woodland Indians to things which proved more sinister—alcohol and firearms. As dependence on these novelties, good and bad, increased, settlers arrived who ushered in yet another innovation, private property. Faced with the puzzling "Pen and Ink work" of purchase or treaty and the less subtle threat of "powder and Ball," no eastern tribe could simply "sit on their mats," with all in turn forced to seek safety in parts "hitherto un-cultivated." Even the powerful Iroquois (Six Nations), the "People of the Longhouse" who could "make the whole New World tremble," knew their time would come. Monacatoocha, the Iroquois envoy to the Shawnee, told his British allies that "you can't live in the woods and be neutral."

As the Indians fought for survival, their reputation (at least to European eyes) as barbaric savages practicing torture and atrocities made it easy to condone a total and devastating war against them. And yet the historical record indicates that Native Americans did not routinely mistreat and murder their prisoners. Indeed, when "rescued," many adoptees desired to continue living with their Indian families, preferring the "savage" way of life. Indian torture of captives, as ghastly as it was, occurred as part of the warriors' complex, and was hardly worse than the treatment meted out by colonists to Native Americans or African slaves on the plantations in the southern colonies or in the West Indies. The European viewpoint was much affected from the beginning by native refusal to become a part of the new society being created. The Indians rejected the role assigned to them of slave, servant, laborer or mercenary. As one historian has observed, "The reluctance of the Indian to adapt himself to colonial civilization was a source of keen disappointment...and was the subject of much comment among the colonists."

Monacatoocha saw danger from French and British alike. For many Indians, but certainly not all, the

Habit of a Mohawk one of the Six Nations, *1757. This Mohawk has the distinctive warrior's hairstyle and is smoking a pipe-tomahawk. Fort Ligonier Association*

An eighteenth century Algonquian pouch of brain-tanned, black-dyed deerskin, bearing a thunderbird image in dyed quillwork. This motif represented to the Indian owner the manito (diety) of the upper world, which was derived from a dream or vision. The pouch, probably Great Lakes in origin, served to hold war and hunting items, tobacco or personal "medicine." Denver Art Museum

French were perceived as the preferable neighbors, perhaps because there were fewer. New France was as "spacious and rich" as any colony in the world, but settlers took little advantage of it. An autocratic and corrupt government at home spawned the same in Canada. There were bright and sensible leaders and a more than competent military force, but immigrants, agriculture and industry were lacking. North America was looked upon by many as a losing financial proposition for the French.

British America had its own problems. The thirteen Atlantic coast colonies were often a quarrelsome lot, unable to cooperate, with each one looking to its own interest. These future United States did, however, have ten times the population of New France and a multitude of merchants, farmers and craftsmen. The society was a magnet for English, Irish, Scots, German, Dutch, French *Huguenot* and even Swedish immigrants. Although a sixty-mile-wide barrier of "endless mountains" made western access a daunting venture, there were numerous backwoodsmen eager to accept the challenge. Irish immigrant George Croghan made a career of offering the natives of the Ohio Valley and Great Lakes his wares, and these tribes increasingly looked to the east—especially Pennsylvania—for their needs, establishing their own priorities and demands for trade goods.

By 1750, the French attempted to reassert their claims, concerned that they were losing the initiative. Just a year before, Captain Pierre-Joseph Céleron de Blainville had led twenty-three canoes and 230 men and traveled 3,000 miles from Montreal through western Pennsylvania and the Ohio country to reestablish authority over supposed French holdings. Burying lead plates at the mouths of major rivers and nailing tin signs to trees that proclaimed the sovereignty of King Louis XV, land title in the region was legitimized in French eyes and contact established with the inhabitants. Indeed, French interests were revitalized and the expedition completed with the loss of only one man. Unfortunately, the French had frequently found opportunistic British traders and indifferent or angry Indians. Far from being optimistic, Céleron de Blainville reported, "all I can say is that the nations of these localities are badly disposed towards the French, and are entirely devoted to the English." It was time to raise the stakes.

10

His Most Christian Majesty Louis XV of France. *National Archives of Canada, C-604*

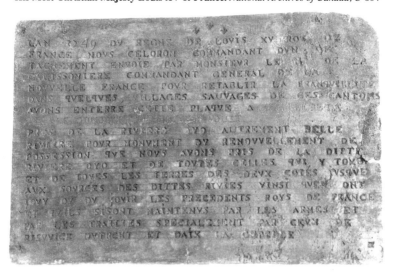

One of the lead plates deposited by Céleron de Blainville in the upper Ohio Valley in 1748, setting forth French claims to the region. Virginia Historical Society

Water routes brought France to western Pennsylvania. Road transport was hazardous and uncertain in the eighteenth century. In America, important cities and transportation routes were tied to the major rivers that flowed inland. To move a single large siege cannon by road and the ammunition to fire it for a day took up to forty horses. To transport the same over water required a single boat of moderate size and a small crew, and, of course, there was no forage problem for a boat.

The fur trade was the principal goal of the French colonies in North America. This endeavor placed a high priority on keeping open the waterways to the south and west, where the pelts were to be found. Denying access to every rival was another important consideration. France secured the entrance to the St. Lawrence River and the Great Lakes system with the fortified towns of Louisbourg and Quebec, and the entrance to the Mississippi River at New Orleans. By tracing the rivers and lakes on a map a great semicircle is drawn, cutting off the British colonies on the Atlantic coast from the immense interior of the continent. By preventing the British from building bases on the Great Lakes or western rivers, the French could stifle both military and commercial competition.

Following Céleron de Blainville's expedition in 1749, the French became increasingly alarmed by commercial activities of British traders in western Pennsylvania and the Ohio country. In 1752, pro-French Ottawa Indians wiped out the British trading post of Pickawillany (modern Piqua, Ohio). The next year the French sent a military force to fortify the significant portages and river junctions in the region. The most important were the Forks of the Ohio, where the Allegheny and Monongahela Rivers joined. The British would never gain access to the river routes without seizing this point. If successful, they could sweep down the Ohio to the west, cutting in half the great French water route linking Canada and Louisiana. Other water communications existed farther west between these two regions, but if the strategic Forks were lost by the French, it was only a matter of time before the weight of British numbers and resources would be felt.

Possession of the rivers enabled the French to move men and supplies into western Pennsylvania each spring, and return them to winter quarters in Canada or French settlements in Illinois each fall. With no more than 1,500 soldiers, they compelled the British to gather several armed forces and spend four years cutting roads over the Allegheny Mountains (suffering several defeats in the process) in attempts to drive them out.

The French forts built for access to and in defense of the Forks of the Ohio—de la Presqu'isle, de la Rivière au Bœuf, Machault, and Duquesne—marked major points on the system of inland water transport. Today, watching a towboat and a dozen heavily laden coal barges moving along almost effortlessly on one of Pittsburgh's rivers, consider what a task it would be to transport the coal by truck over the mountains on the Pennsylvania Turnpike.

Two French cannon shot of iron, marked with the fleur-de-lis. Pennsylvania Historical and Museum Commission

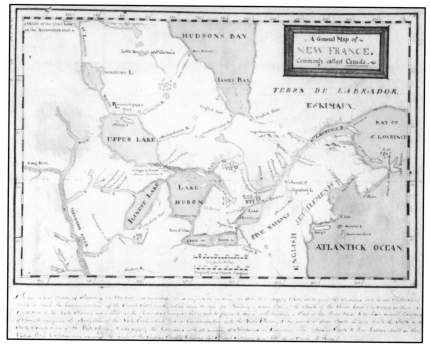

A General Map of New France. Commonly called Canada. *This wartime map shows the great advantage held by the French in North America, an extensive chain of rivers and lakes on which to travel. British Library*

"I was commissioned to visit and deliver a letter to the commandant of the French forces on the Ohio . . . ."
   Major George Washington, 1753

Part 2

George Washington Loses a Battle and Starts a War: Great Meadows, 1754

Ange de Menneville, Marquis de Duquesne, *the Governor of New France, after whom Fort Duquesne was named.* National Archives of Canada, C-84058

Captain Céleron de Blainville helped to rekindle interest in the thousand-mile highway the French called *La Belle Rivière,* the Beautiful River. Suddenly, the Ohio, which had scarcely graced a map a generation earlier, began to attract traders, settlers and Indians alike. A fortified settlement near the strategic Forks, where the Monongahela joined the Allegheny, would help control access to the Ohio Valley.

Ange de Menneville, Marquis de Duquesne, the Governor of New France, launched his bid for the Ohio from Montreal in the summer of 1753. The lakes and rivers dictated the route and the French leapfrogged their men and supplies, building forts at strategic or commercial points. Following the water route through the St. Lawrence River, Lake Ontario, the Niagara River and Lake Erie, the first fort, de la Presqu'isle (modern Erie, Pennsylvania), was erected after which they dragged and carried supplies over twenty-one miles of tortuous terrain to the next fort, de la Rivière au Boeuf (modern Waterford, Pennsylvania). By winter, after backbreaking efforts that took a heavy toll of personnel, the expedition withdrew to Montreal. The chain of forts to the Ohio could not be completed until spring.

As a small French garrison settled in for winter at Fort de la Rivière au Boeuf, a young Anglo-American visitor suddenly appeared with a letter from the Lieutenant Governor of Virginia. "By whose authority," the letter read, "[have the French] invaded the King of Great Britain's territories? It becomes my duty to require your peaceable departure." The fort commander, astounded and bemused by this bravado, politely sent the Virginian south with the only possible answer, "As to the summons you send me to retire, I do not think myself obliged to obey." The Virginia Lieutenant Governor's seemingly hollow threat, however, had its effect. By February, the French were dragging more supplies over the frozen Great Lakes. On April 16, 1754, 360 canoes and flat-bottomed bateaux arrived at the Forks of the Ohio to stake His Most Christian Majesty's (the King of France's) claim to the valley. Forty Virginia militiamen were already there building a fortified log storehouse. Outnumbered twelve to one, the Virginians were sent packing "with great civility." Work began immediately on a proper stronghold, Fort Duquesne.

Twenty-one-year-old provincial major, George Washington, was in the midst of the first great exploit of his remarkable career. Ambitious and eager to become a material player in the diplomatic process, he had leaped at the opportunity in 1753 to be emissary to the French

Robert Dinwiddie *(artist and date unknown), Lieutenant Governor of Virginia, perceived a French challenge beyond the Alleghenies, sending Washington on his famous mission to the Ohio in 1753. The National Portrait Gallery, London*

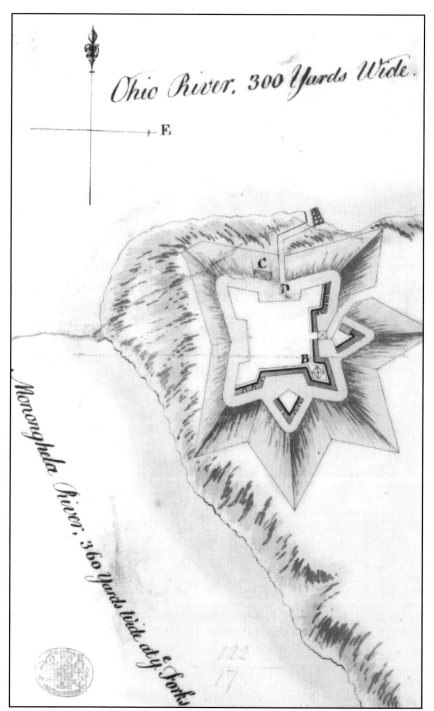

Ohio River, 300 Yards Wide.

E

C
D
B

Monongahela River, 360 Yards Wide at ỹ Forks

122
17

Fort Duquesne in 1758 by a British army engineer. British Library

Washington drew this map of his 1753-1754 journey to the Ohio after his return to Williamsburg. It is based on field notes, compass readings and impressions of what he had viewed. British Library

for Virginia Lieutenant Governor Robert Dinwiddie. The Virginians had a special interest in the Ohio Valley. As enterprising American speculators carved up great parcels of the vaguely charted territory for future settlement and exploitation, Virginia and London businessmen formed the Ohio Company. The British Crown promised the company up to 500,000 acres if it would find the means to establish a foothold. Knowing that the French had other plans, the Lieutenant Governor wanted to show the world that Virginia settlers belonged in the western lands.

Major Washington was the willing instrument of Dinwiddie's strategy. Young, eager and inexperienced, he and the veteran trader Christopher Gist plunged impetuously into the wilderness. Washington's thousand-mile winter mission from Williamsburg to Fort de la Rivière au Boeuf in 1753 had enough drama to fill a lifetime. He was shot at by hostile Indians, almost drowned when he fell into the icy Allegheny River, and spent many weeks shivering through mountain blizzards. Through it all, he cooly kept a journal that described the Forks of the Ohio as "extremely well situated for a fort," observed the mood of the native inhabitants, mapped the path of his journey and assessed the strength of French forts. The Virginia Lieutenant Governor was so delighted with Washington's report that he had it published and sent to Europe. London and Paris soon would learn of George Washington.

King George II still had "an utter aversion" to committing British troops to a purely colonial dilemma. He sent funds but instructed Virginia to look to its neighboring colonies for assistance, which Dinwiddie attempted to do. With the spring thaw of 1754, newly promoted Lieutenant Colonel Washington headed west with 132 "self-willed and ungovernable" troops who had been promised free land in the Ohio Valley. Dinwiddie had extracted pledges of funds, professional soldiers, wagons, horses and a thousand Cherokee and Catawba Indians from the Carolinas.

In April, as the Virginians marched from Winchester to Wills Creek (Cumberland, Maryland), none of the news was good. No wagons, horses, troops or native allies were anywhere in evidence. Word was received that a large French force was building a substantial fort at the Forks of the Ohio. Those familiar with the backwoods predicted that no road could ever be built over the mountains. Washington, huddling with his officers, decided to try to cut a hundred-mile road over the Nemacolin Path that had been blazed for the

His Majesty King George II of Great Britain *by Thomas Hudson, 1744. The National Portrait Gallery, London*

19

This gilded brass gorget was worn by George Washington as part of his uniform as a Virginia provincial officer. It bears the colonial arms of Virginia, including the Latin Motto: **En Dat Virginia Quartam** *(Behold! Virginia Yields the Fourth). The motto referred to Virginia as the fourth kingdom of the British empire after England, Scotland and Ireland. This half-moon shaped metal insignia represented the last vestige of medieval armor, and at this time was regulation in the British army. Engraved with the King's arms or the King's cypher and crown, or as in this case the arms of an American colony, it was no longer defensive armor but merely a lightweight, ornamental symbol of rank for commissioned officers. It was worn around the neck suspended by a ribbon. Massachusetts Historical Society*

Ohio Company. Once they reached the Monongahela River, they would wait for reinforcements as well as artillery to reduce the new French fort. The Virginian wanted to "preserve our men from the sorry consequences of inaction and encourage our Indian allies."

Thus began the first of several treks over the Allegheny Mountains. There simply was no shortcut. Washington explored the nearby Youghiogheny River for a water passage and found a fall (Ohiopyle) that even prevented the movement of canoes. All through the month of May, the men, perhaps wondering why they had willingly volunteered for such hardship, chopped and hacked their way over the slopes. Finally, they found a mile-long opening called the Great Meadows. As the troops set up a temporary field camp and cut forage for the animals, Washington, looking at it from a military and topographic vantage point, described this spot as a "charming field for an encounter."

On May 27, the Virginians made contact with Christopher Gist. He informed them that a party of fifty French soldiers was only a few miles away. Tanacharison, the "Half King," a Mingo (Iroquois) who represented Six Nations' interests in the region, relayed that he knew the foe's whereabouts to Washington, who with forty soldiers stumbled through darkness and heavy rain to the camp of this most important local Indian ally. At sunrise, Tanacharison and Monacatoocha took them to the French camp where a fifteen-minute fight ensued. It was unclear what caused the first shot. Ten French were lost, including Ensign Joseph Coulon de Villiers, Sieur de Jumonville, and twenty-one were captured (one also escaped). A sole Virginian was slain. Washington was ecstatic over his victory. The French would call it an unprovoked ambush but Washington was certain that Ensign Villiers de Jumonville and his force were skulking about planning to attack the British. It also began to dawn on the Virginia commander that the French might be back soon in considerable force. He returned to the Great Meadows and erected a circular palisade, two-thirds of it covered by trenches, that he saw as a "fort of necessity." In Williamsburg, a nervous Dinwiddie rationalized in a later report to the London ministers that the "little skirmish was really the work of the Half King and...Indians. We were as auxiliaries to them."

In June, some reinforcements from Virginia and South Carolina arrived, bringing the British force to 400. However, these troops, an Independent Company of regulars from South Carolina under Captain James

Thirteenth Regt. of Foot. Corporal Jones. Drawn by Lieutenant William Baillie whilst on the Recruiting Service at Birmingham in the Year 1753. *This drawing depicts the British infantry soldier as he actually looked on the eve of war with France. Typically, the clothing is well fitted and also well worn. The hat is "cocked" and turned at an angle to allow the shouldering of his musket on the left side during drill. Light Infantry Museum, Taunton*

Peter Manigault & His Friends, *artist unknown, circa 1760. This drawing shows officers of the Independent Company stationed in Charleston, South Carolina. The Henry Francis du Pont Winterthur Museum*

McKay, were professional soldiers and refused to participate in such a menial task as constructing a road without extra pay. An exasperated Washington, resupplied with some sixty head of cattle, flour and six swivel guns (small, portable cannon), continued his road building toward the Monongahela. The next stop, beyond the steep slope of Chestnut Ridge, was Christopher Gist's plantation where the Ohio Company had anticipated settling 150 families. At Gist's, the British tried without success to cajole and then threaten local Indians into helping them. Only Tanacharison and ancient Seneca "Queen" Aliquippa had joined the troops at Fort Necessity. The Indians encamped with Washington—mostly women, children and old men—were consuming the dwindling supplies of food. As rumors spread that a large French force was leaving Fort Duquesne to avenge Jumonville Glen, even these dubious allies drifted away into the woods.

The rumors were true. Six hundred French troops and militia, accompanied by a hundred-man native contingent, headed south from Fort Duquesne on June 28. The commander, Captain Louis Coulon de Villiers, was the brother (or half brother) of the dead Villiers de Jumonville. The British, thirteen miles from Fort Necessity on road construction duty, scurried back to the haven at the Great Meadows. By the time they arrived on July 1, a hundred men were too sick and weak to continue work on the palisade and trenches. Without supplies, food or reinforcements the miserable little army prepared for the worst. Now that their lives were at stake, the haughty Independent Company worked feverishly with everyone else to strengthen the defenses.

The French column, warily reacting to a report that a 5,000(!)-man enemy force was close by, did not arrive until the third of July. British attempts to lure their opponents out into a formal clash on the meadow failed, and a siege began in a steady rain. The men in the trenches and the stockade were a concentrated target as "The Enemy [was] galling us on all sides incessantly from the woods." Toward evening, "The most tremendous rain that can be conceived...set everything afloat" and all firing ceased. By sunset, the British had thirty-one dead and seventy wounded lying in knee-deep mud and water. Even before firing had ceased some of the distressed men had discovered a rum supply inside the stockade, making a grievous situation even worse.

Suddenly the French asked for a parley. Washington, desperate but "expecting a deceit," agreed. Captain Coulon de Villiers was having his own problems with soldiers and Indians threatening to desert, so he offered the British the chance to leave their fort with the honors of war. He was also quick to point out that he might not be able to control his native allies if the garrison did not surrender. A disconcerted Washington did not concur with the first verbal terms proposed by his adversaries, so he instructed his interpreter to go back for another parley. After this second set of negotiations, the interpreter returned with formal written terms. With no real choice, he and Captain McKay finally signed the documents at midnight. The next morning, having promised to stay east of the mountains for a year, the humbled forces of the British Crown left two hostages, as stipulated in the surrender, and limped back over the wilderness path for five days to Wills Creek. The surrender date was July 4, 1754.

The French now occupied a commanding position in the Ohio Valley. Colonel Washington, returned to the Virginia Tidewater and reporting to Lieutenant Governor Dinwiddie, found to his astonishment that he had signed a surrender document stating that he had *assassinated* Ensign Villiers de Jumonville. Criticized for his performance on the frontier, he resigned his commission and returned to the role of "gentleman farmer" at Mount Vernon.

George Washington *by Charles Willson Peale, circa 1772. He is uniformed and armed as a Virginia provincial officer in 1758. Washington/ Custis/Lee Collection, Washington and Lee University*

The flintlock apparatus of a model 1728 French musket, the type of shoulder arm carried by the Independent Companies of Marine Infantry. Old Fort Niagara Association

Between 1753 and 1759 the French garrisons posted to western Pennsylvania consisted of Canadian militia and *Compagnies Franches de la Marine* (Independent Companies of Marine Infantry). French colonies, including New France (Canada) and Louisiana, were under the Marine Ministry (Navy), which provided Marine companies as regular forces. Not until 1755, when four battalions arrived, were any regular French army units sent to Canada. None came farther south or west than Niagara.

Virtually all soldiers in the *Compagnies Franches* were sent from France, the Canadian population being too sparse to provide recruits. Most of the officers were Canadian. Thirty companies were stationed in New France when war broke out. Every company could serve as a separate unit, under the authority of the Governor-General, who was responsible to the Minister of Marine. Company size was set at a captain, a lieutenant, an ensign, two sergeants, four corporals, two drummers, one fifer and between twenty-nine and sixty soldiers. Several cadets—young officer candidates—might also be included.

All adult males in Canada were required to serve in the militia. They provided their own clothing and arms, usually smoothbore hunting weapons. The militia was often used for physical labor, and was skilled in transport duties with boats and canoes.

Marines and militia often fought in the field as detachments of men from different companies. These mixed units could give a good account of themselves if they did not have to face in the open field larger, better-trained units. The Canadian officers were brave if often untaught in routine military duties, and their troops were known as accurate marksmen. When Braddock was defeated in 1755, for instance, a force of 100 marines under Captain Dumas stood fast long enough for the militia and Indians to envelop the British flanks and open a protected fire on the enemy. In 1759 though, in an attempt to drive the British away from the siege of Fort Niagara, the officers rashly led a force of marines and militia in a headlong charge against the British standing in line of battle. The massed firepower from sustained regular enemy volleys devastated the French attack, and both officers and men lacked the discipline to form into line and return fire. They were driven from the field, and the French force that might have saved Niagara and then retaken Pittsburgh from the British was destroyed.

A French military field drum painted with a version of the French coat of arms (ropes are reproduction). J. Craig Nannos Collection

"We have lost gallant officers and generous friends, not in battle . . . but by murder, by savage butchery."
Lieutenant Matthew Leslie, 1755

Part 3

General Braddock Builds a Road to Disaster: The Monongahela, 1755

His Royal Highness William Augustus, the Duke of Cumberland *by Sir Joshua Reynolds, circa 1758-1760. The younger son of King George II, Cumberland fought the French in numerous battles, but earned the sobriquet "butcher" for his ruthless suppression of the Scottish rising of 1745-1746. He was a competent administrator and planner, and a successful military reformer. But his acceptance of the Convention of Kloster-Seven in 1757, leading to the disbanding of his command in Germany, caused his dismissal as Captain General of the British army. The National Portrait Gallery, London*

The struggle for the Ohio paused only while the British decided how best to drive the French from the valley. The Duke of Cumberland, war hero and son of King George II, prepared a plan to win this war before it was ever declared. A 3,500-man army with siege artillery would cross the mountains and reduce Fort Duquesne in the spring of 1755. From there it would march north with the objective of seizing Fort Niagara. Logistics would be difficult, but Fort Duquesne was the symbol of French *hauteur* and it had to be replaced by a British fort at the Forks.

Edward Braddock, sixty, a forty-five-year Coldstream Guard veteran, commanded the new expedition. Two 500-man infantry units, the Forty-fourth and Forty-eighth Regiments of Foot, and nineteen artillery pieces sailed from Ireland with a twenty-ship convoy in January of 1755. When they entered the Chesapeake Bay in March, Braddock was already behind schedule, and he labored mightily to gather the promised men and supplies from the Americans. The usual frictions between the British and their colonial allies surfaced immediately. At a meeting in Alexandria, provincial leaders argued for bypassing the Ohio and pursuing an easier New York campaign against Fort Niagara—strangling the French lifeline to the west. Braddock, however, had his orders and was not interested in a debate. He would use Wills Creek, rechristened Fort Cumberland in honor of the Duke, as his strategic base of operations. Improving the 1754 road cut by the Virginians, he intended to move as rapidly as possible to cross the Alleghenies, capture Fort Duquesne, and head to the north. Mindful of the need for colonial experience, he added the not unenthusiastic veteran George Washington as his aide.

By May 10, the General, traveling over a road "almost uninhabited, but by a parcel of Banditti who call themselves Indian traders," arrived with his party at Fort Cumberland. A woman in the expedition called the fort "the most desolate Place" she had ever seen. Not without cause, Braddock fumed and fussed over the "very indifferent" quality of his provincial recruits, the greed of his contractors and the scarcity of every type of supply. He then proceeded to lose his valuable native allies due to his disciplinary action of ordering away the Indian women, which in turn caused the indignant men to leave also. His quartermaster, the controversial Scotsman Sir John St. Clair, spent much of his time quarreling with the Americans. The frustration grew, although the distant but effective assistance of the resourceful Pennsylvanian Benjamin Franklin resulted in the arrival at the fort of 150 wagons and 500 horses. Braddock commented that Pennsylvania had "promised nothing and performed everything" while the rest of the colonies had "promised everything and performed nothing."

After a tense month of preparations at Fort Cumberland, the 2,200-man army received its marching orders to move on June 9. The British were six weeks behind schedule, but they had used the time to train the most potent military force (on paper) North America had ever seen. A slight majority of the thousand men of the understrength Forty-fourth and Forty-eighth Regiments were actually British draftees and American recruits. There were also some 500 other troops: Independent Companies from New York and South Carolina, and provincials from Maryland, Virginia and North Carolina. Serving as the "eyes" of the army was a small detachment of "light horse" (cavalry). A large corps of axemen went ahead of the main body chopping a road through the immense forest. Thirty sailors accompanied the force to assist in dragging the cumbersome siege artillery over the mountains. Only eight Indians, however, out of a much larger number originally enlisted, remained to assist as scouts in the woods. After ten days, the five-mile-long column had inched only twenty-six miles. Worried by his dwindling food supply and rumors of French reinforcements at the Forks, Braddock, on Washington's advice, created a "flying column" of 1,300 men with a few pieces of artillery, leaving most of the wagons, heavy equipment and the rest of the army trailing behind. The new tactic worked. Within twenty more days, the advance party had hacked a twelve-foot-wide path the many miles to the banks of the Monongahela. On July 9, they "hugged themselves for joy" and played their fifes and drums to the tune of "The Grenadiers March" as the splendid force forded the river only a few miles from Fort Duquesne. George Washington, so sick and weak from dysentery that he could hardly ride a horse but mightily impressed by the appearance of this armed host, insisted on being with the troops as they captured the "highest object of their wishes."

Where were the French? Fort commander Captain Claude Pierre Pécaudy, Sieur de Contrecoeur, had 600 troops and 800 Indians waiting at the Forks. Local Shawnee, Delaware and Iroquois were there, but the great majority were "French Indians," including the

Sir John St. Clair, *miniature by John Singleton Copley, circa 1758, served in North America from 1755 to 1767. He was a major in the Twenty-second Regiment of Foot and in 1754 was selected for the much prized office of Deputy Quarter Master General for the British forces in Pennsylvania. His self-proclaimed status as a Scottish baronet has never been substantiated. Lieutenant Governor Dinwiddie observed that he possessed "much Merit & great Knowledge in Military Affairs." Historical Society of Pennsylvania*

This British officer's sash, owned by General Braddock, was woven of scarlet silk, twelve feet long and thirty inches wide, terminated with tassels. Embroidered into the open mesh above the row of standing figures was the date 1709, the year (old style) that Braddock's father–like his son also of the Coldstream Guards–received his commission from Queen Anne as a major general. On July 9, 1755, after Braddock was fatally wounded, this sash was reportedly removed from over his shoulder and the silk net stretched and expanded to its full length, to serve its ultimate purpose as a litter. Braddock was carried in it from the field and placed in a cart for the retreat back to Dunbar's Camp. Four days later he succumbed near Fort Necessity and Washington came into possession of the sash, probably as a bequest from the dying Braddock. Mount Vernon Ladies Association

Grenadiers. 46th, 47th, 48th Regiments *by David Morier, circa 1751. This detail shows a private of the grenadier company, Forty-eighth Regiment of Foot. This unit was one of two regular British battalions in Braddock's army. Grenadiers were picked troops who originally hurled grenades. By 1755, they no longer carried grenades but still represented the strongest and bravest infantrymen in a regiment. The distinctive cap or miter was the emblem of these special soldiers. After Braddock's defeat the Indians were seen bringing in grenadier's caps at Fort Duquesne as part of their booty. Her Majesty Queen Elizabeth II*

Captain Daniel-Hyacinthe-Marie Liénard de Beaujeu of the Independent Company of Marine Infantry. Engraving by J.A. O'Neill, Pf 984.4. Musée du Séminaire de Québec

skilled Wyandot, Ottawa and Potawatomi from the Great Lakes. Even without many of his Indians, Braddock had protected his column too well to be attacked as it approached the Ohio. Knowing that he could not defend his wooden fort against the overwhelming troops and artillery, Pécaudy de Contrecoeur weighed unpleasant options. Captain Daniel-Hyacinthe-Marie Liénard de Beaujeu, just arrived from Quebec to take command, argued for a headlong assault on the British while they were still in the forest. The warriors, however, were not enthusiastic about a pitched battle. A month short of his forty-fifth birthday, the audacious Liénard de Beaujeu, stripped to the waist and an officer's gorget around his neck, used all of his years of frontier experience to coax the Indians into an attack. On the morning of July 9, some 250 soldiers and 600 Native Americans ran east into the woods to blunt the British advance.

What happened next was one of the great paradoxes of American history. Full of optimism, the British, so near their goal after weeks of hard work and trepidation, temporarily let down their guard. The head of the column under Major Thomas Gage collided with the French and Indians—a surprise for each side—and Captain Liénard de Beaujeu was killed in the first volleys. At that moment, the French might have decided that fate was against them, but another officer, Captain Jean-Daniel Dumas, stepped in and directed his command to fan out down both sides of the road in a "half-moon" formation, with the aim of flanking and then surrounding the British. A panicky Gage soon retreated, abandoning two field pieces, which the French turned onto their former owners. As the troops in the rear rushed to the firing, they ran into those streaming back from the front. The Redcoat column telescoped, turning into a mass of frightened men which a modern historian has characterized as a "red bullseye." Order evaporating, the shocked troops ignored their superiors and bunched together under an appalling fire, too fearful to fire *and* move against the enemy. The British suffered nearly one thousand casualties in two hours fighting an enemy sheltered by trees and occupying a commanding hill. Over sixty officers were hit while trying in vain to contain the disorder and reinstill discipline. General Braddock was later much criticized for failing to modify his tactics for the conditions of the American wilderness. This charge was unfair because whatever dispositions he may have contemplated to counter the French and Indians, it proved impossible in the chaos on the road to execute them. The General showed great bravery in his first real battle. After having four horses shot from under him, he was hit in the lungs and carried from the field in his sash. George Washington, with the extraordinary luck that to many cast about him an aura of divinity, was on horseback in the thick of the fighting but did not receive a scratch.

The rout was complete. Men "broke and ran as sheep before hounds." The survivors were panic-stricken with dread of Indian capture, and stampeded for safety across the Monongahela. General Braddock, who might have been a great hero, was nothing but a dead scapegoat. A few days later he was buried anonymously on the wilderness road that bore his name near the deserted Fort Necessity. The other segment of the British army, still capable of attacking the fort, was so terrorized that its new commander, Colonel Thomas Dunbar, immediately marched the entire force east to Philadelphia and set up winter quarters in July. Totally frustrated, Lieutenant Governor Dinwiddie commented that this Colonel "appears to have determined to leave our frontiers as defenseless as possible."

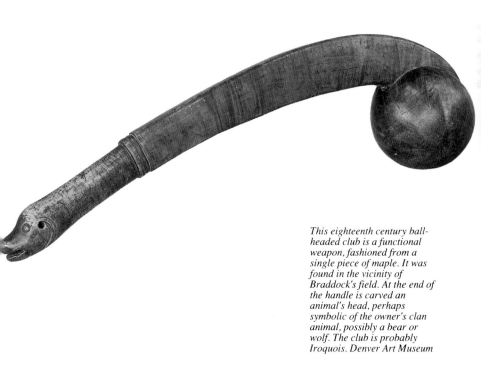

This eighteenth century ball-headed club is a functional weapon, fashioned from a single piece of maple. It was found in the vicinity of Braddock's field. At the end of the handle is carved an animal's head, perhaps symbolic of the owner's clan animal, possibly a bear or wolf. The club is probably Iroquois. Denver Art Museum

Glasgow Green, *artist unknown, circa 1756-1758. Perhaps the most famous unit to serve in western Pennsylvania during the conflict can be seen here, the Forty-second Regiment of Foot, also known as the Royal Highland Regiment after 1758. The somber blue-green tones of the tartan worn by the men gave rise to the appellation "Black Watch." This battalion of the Forty-second is in column*

In the course of the war for empire in western Pennsylvania (1754-1764), several distinct types of armed fighting men served the British Crown. The expeditionary armies and frontier defenses contained a mixture of civilian militia, provincial troops, Independent Companies and British regulars.

The militia was generally composed of all able-bodied, free white men in the colony who were required by law to maintain arms and attend periodic training. Part of George Washington's Virginia Regiment at Fort Necessity in 1754 was drawn from that colony's militia, and militia units in the frontier counties played an important role in constructing and garrisoning fortifications. Pennsylvania had no militia law before 1755, and relied heavily on volunteers paid by the colony to construct and maintain its frontier defenses. During the Indian War of 1763-1764, militia companies drawn from the civilian inhabitants of the military posts in the region helped to defend such forts as Pitt, Ligonier and Bedford.

Provincial troops consisted of volunteers who were recruited, equipped and paid by individual colonies. They were enlisted for a specific period of time, usually one to three years, and unlike the militia were permitted to serve outside the borders of their respective colonies. At various times from 1754-1764, Pennsylvania, Virginia, Maryland the "lower counties" (modern Delaware),and North Carolina sent provincial forces into western Pennsylvania.

formation, maneuvering and firing by platoons. Drummers are posted to the left, halberds (polearms) carried by sergeants are visible in each platoon, officers are overseeing the movements and the regimental colors are displayed at the center of the column. The Trustees of the Black Watch Regimental Museum

Independent Companies were units of the British regular army dispatched from England to garrison fortifications in colonial cities and towns, primarily on the coast. They were seldom drawn from the fittest elements of the regular army. Long supply lines and relative isolation from inspecting officers did little to enhance the condition of the corps, and thus their clothing, arms and equipment were often in poor repair or completely worn out. Independent Companies served with Washington at Fort Necessity in 1754 and Braddock in 1755.

Between the outbreak of hostilities in 1754 and the end of the Indian War in 1764, various elements of the Forty-second (Black Watch), Forty-fourth, Forty-eighth, Fiftieth, Sixtieth (Royal Ameri-can Regiment), Seventy-seventh (Montgomery's Highlanders) and Ninety-fourth (Royal Welsh Volunteers) Regiments served in the region. These troops were paid by the Crown and were generally raised in the British Isles, although thousands of colonials enlisted in the regular army during the war. Individuals were often drafted out of the militia to complete provincial and regular regiments, and there appears to have been a great deal of movement among the regiments raised by the various provinces and the regular army.

"I have succeeded in ruining the three adjacent provinces, Pennsylvania, Maryland, and Virginia, driving off the inhabitants, and totally destroying their settlements . . . ."

Captain Jean-Daniel Dumas, 1756

Part 4

The French and Indian Offensive: 1755-58

An eighteenth century Indian trade armband of silver, engraved with a totem of a fish.
Fort Ligonier Association

The French were restrained as they counted the spoils of their unexpected victory. They realized how easily the verdict could have favored the British. What would have been the result, for example, if Gage and his vanguard had pushed forward instead of lapsing into disorganized retreat? After several days of frenzied scalping, looting and torture, the Indians left the enemy dead to decompose on Braddock's Field and returned to their villages. Robbed of his elusive goal for the second time, George Washington trembled "at the consequences this defeat may have upon our back [country] settlers."

By October of 1755, the fear that was such a familiar part of frontier life was spreading east and south across the Allegheny Mountains. The French and Indian scalping parties intended to "kill, burn, scalp, destroy, and spread terror in every direction." Without British armies, and with few colonial troops (mainly Washington's Virginia Regiment) brave enough to search the forests for the enemy, the settlers were forced to flee to the east or turn their log homes into fortified blockhouses. The tactics were as old as the New World settlements. This type native warfare—*petite guerre*—featured small numbers, swiftness, mobility and destruction, and had the effect of harrowing the enemy, both soldiers and civilians. French-led parties of Indians would strike suddenly at dawn, burning houses, butchering horses and cattle, and frequently killing and scalping, or if possible, dragging away men, women and children alike to be adopted into a tribe to replenish dwindling populations.

In an attempt to counter this problem, Pennsylvania policy called for the erection of a line of small forts along the frontiers during the first half of 1756, but this defense system soon proved ineffective in curtailing the raids. One of the posts, Fort Granville, was actually besieged and captured on July 30 by the influential Delaware war chief Captain Jacobs and a French-native force. In retaliation, Pennsylvania Colonel John Armstrong made plans to strike back from another post in the defensive line, Fort Shirley. In September he led a secret mission to destroy the Delaware stronghold of Kittanning on the Allegheny River. The largest Indian town in western Pennsylvania, Kittanning, home of Captain Jacobs, was a center for housing prisoners, and the storehouse and base for launching *petite guerre* against the settlements. Armstrong's 300 Pennsylvanians suffered heavy casualties but surprised this community of perhaps a hundred warriors and a few French soldiers, killing in the process Captain Jacobs.

Habit of a Delaware Indian with his Tomohawk Scalping Knife, *1757. This Delaware is attired in a feather headdress and the toga-like "matchcoat."*
Fort Ligonier Association

The silver medal struck to commemorate Armstrong's expedition against Kittanning. It reads (left) **The Gift Of The Corporation Of The City Of Philadelphia** *and (right)* **Kittanning Destroyed By Coll. Armstrong. September. 8. 1756.** *Historical Society of Pennsylvania*

A handful of prisoners was liberated. This action was only a partial success, but as a consequence morale on the frontier was lifted and the Corporation of the City of Philadelphia was impressed enough to have a special victory medal struck. Kittanning itself was abandoned. The long-term futility of this punitive expedition soon became evident though, and by 1757 French-Indian raiding had destroyed hundreds of dwellings as far east as the valley of the Susquehanna River. The French boasted that they had succeeded in "ruining the three adjacent provinces, Pennsylvania, Maryland, and Virginia...."

Quaker-controlled Pennsylvania, long committed to an "orderly society" and peaceful relations with the Indians, was unprepared for the onslaught. A Virginian gave some unsought advice to his frightened neighbors, "The pacifick gentlemen of your country will either change their principles, or have their throats cut." Under increasing pressure, the old Quaker pacifism was modified in part as Pennsylvania completed the chain of forts and began to enlist soldiers to stem the tide. Yet as shall be seen, the Quakers' efforts at promoting harmony would play a decisive part in the coming campaign of 1758. Non-Quaker Ben Franklin, always the pragmatist, was a principal actor in the "military business," all the while complaining that "I [do] not conceive myself qualified for it."

In the 1750's the vast territory between the Allegheny Mountains and the Mississippi River held a diverse range of indigenous peoples: the Iroquois, the Algonquians and the Southern nations.

The Indians in the north were divided essentially by language. The Iroquois, living in modern New York State, western Pennsylvania and Ohio, were composed of the Mohawk, Oneida, Onondaga, Cayuga, and Seneca. A southern Iroquoian tribe, the Tuscarora, joined the League of the Iroquois as a junior partner in the early 1700's, thereby creating the "Six Nations." Though the League was officially neutral, it was generally aligned with the British. On the other hand, the Seneca (western-most nation) expressed considerable pro-French sentiment and were extremely active in assaulting the New York and Pennsylvania frontiers during the Indian war of 1763-1764. Those Iroquois who colonized the upper Ohio Valley region were known as the Mingo. There were two Iroquoian groups that sided with the French: the Wyandot, who occupied the Detroit and Lake Erie areas and the Caughnawaga (French Mohawk) of Canada. By the 1750's some bands of this latter group had relocated to Ohio.

The Algonquian peoples were situated in the lands between the Ohio River and the Great Lakes. These tribes— Ottawa, Potawatomi, Ojibwa (Chippewa), Sauk-Fox, Illinois, Kickapoo, Miami, Shawnee and Delaware—represented a sizeable percentage of France's Indian allies fighting in the western Pennsylvania region. They were joined by other Native Americans from Canada, many of whom were converts to Christianity and resolute in devotion to New France. That was not the case for the Shawnee and Delaware of Ohio, who defected from the French after the 1758 Treaty of Easton. But by 1763 most of the Algonquian peoples, including the Ohio Indians, offered bitter resistance to the British and Americans.

The Southern Indians, the Cherokee and Catawba, played a peripheral role in the fighting in western Pennsylvania. Their traditional enmity for the Northern Algonquian nations was such that they offered their services as allies to the British in the Braddock and Forbes campaigns. That proved largely unsuccessful, and in the closing days of the conflict the Cherokee found themselves at war with the Anglo-Americans.

"I have often heard the British officers call the Indians undisciplined savages, which is a capital mistake—" so wrote James Smith, captured by Ohio Indians near Raystown just before Braddock's defeat. He lived with the Caughnawaga for several years as an adoptee and gained a singular perspective into the Woodland peoples' military capabilities. The warriors, he observed, "have all the essentials of discipline. They are under good command, and punctual in obeying orders: they can act in concert....When they go into battle they are not loaded or encumbered with many clothes, as they commonly fight naked, save only breech-clout, leggins and mockesons....Could it be supposed that undisciplined troops could defeat Generals Braddock, Grant & c.? It may be said by some that the French were also engaged in this war: true, they were; yet I know it was the Indians that laid the plan, and with small assistance, put it into execution."

The success of the Indians in their wilderness warfare is all the more extraordinary when it is recognized that the woodland stretches beyond the Alleghenies held only a scant native population in this period. For almost a decade a few thousand native warriors dominated the frontiers of the British colonies that were populated by well over a million inhabitants.

An Indian of the Outawas Tribe & his Family going to War *and* **An Indian War chief compleatly equipped with a scalp in his hand.** *These drawings of Woodland Indians were sketched from life by British officer George Townshend, circa 1759. The National Trust Photographic Library*

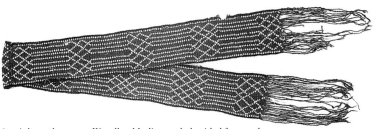

An eighteenth century Woodland Indian sash, braided from red trade yarn and white beads. Denver Art Museum

43

"Why don't [the British] and French fight on the sea? [They] come here only to cheat the poor Indians, and take their land from them."
        Shamokin Daniel, a Delaware, 1758

Part 5

General Forbes Builds a New Route to Victory: The Forbes Road, 1758

"This part of the world does not abound in good news." A British general was grumbling about reverses in 1756, but he just as well could have been describing the entire four years of British defeat and humiliation that had begun at the Great Meadows in 1754. All the efforts, expense and loss of lives had gained nothing. The French and their Indian allies had victories and scalps too numerous to count from New York to the Carolinas. They knew, however, that their successes had not won the war. In fact, General Louis-Joseph, Marquis de Montcalm-Gozon de Saint Véran actually saw his New France slowly being overwhelmed by British supplies and troops, lamenting, "We are resolved to bury ourselves under the ruins of the colony."

The undeclared conflict had become official in 1756, eventually to be known as the Seven Years War. North America, rich in potential, became an important phase in a world war for empire, but was always secondary to European priorities. The British, for all their mistakes, were determined to achieve victory in every theater.

Good news for the Americans finally began to arrive in 1757. One of Great Britain's notable civilian leaders, Secretary of State William Pitt, had come to power. With pluck and tenacity, he began to reverse British fortunes and help mold the small island country into the world's greatest power. With General John Ligonier as his chief military advisor (he had replaced the Duke of Cumberland, now in disgrace for his misconduct of the war in Germany), Pitt took charge of the war. He formulated a three-pronged attack on New France for the 1758 season. While other forces under General Jeffery Amherst were to attack Fortress Louisbourg near the mouth of the St. Lawrence River, and General James Abercromby was assigned to take Fort Ticonderoga on Lake Champlain, a third expedition would again scale the mountains barring the way to the Ohio Valley.

Sagacious leaders were chosen to lead the attack on Fort Duquesne. The choices, in fact, made possible its success. Fifty-year-old Brigadier General John Forbes, a Scot, had studied medicine before entering the army in 1735. He had been a staff officer with Ligonier and had served under the British commander in North America, John Campbell, Earl of Loudoun. His superb skills as an administrator would be put to the test on the Pennsylvania frontier. Colonel Henry Bouquet, a thirty-nine-year-old Protestant Swiss, had seen active service in the

William Pitt, later the First Earl of Chatham, by William Hoare, 1754. As Secretary of State, Pitt was the dominant figure in the war effort against France. General Forbes renamed Fort Duquesne "Pittsburgh" in his honor. The National Portrait Gallery, London

The chamber bagpipes of Colonel Archibald Montgomery (or Montgomerie). Formerly of the Scots Greys Regiment, he commanded the First Highland Battalion, raised in 1757, in the Forbes campaign. The unit was also known as Montgomery's Highlanders, or the Sixty-second Foot and later the Seventy-seventh Foot, reflecting the confusing renaming and renumbering of regiments during the war. It had been realized by the British Government that Scottish troops could be useful in America, and a survey of the Highlands in the 1750's indicated that the population included some 12,000 eligible young men. Scottish landowners were more than willing to ingratiate themselves with authorities in wake of the Jacobite Rising of 1745-1746, in which many lost their property. Then too, with the distinct possibility of a French invasion of Britain starting in 1756, the removal of armed, potential rebels from the Highlands and their transporting to America made good, if not cynical, sense.

The thirty-two-year-old Montgomery, later Earl of Eglinton, was reported to be an able, hot-tempered and hard-drinking figure. After the Forbes campaign he served under Amherst in New York. In 1760 he was placed in command of an expeditionary force directed against the Cherokee Indians in South Carolina. Two years later he was elevated to the rank of colonel in the regular British army. Unfortunately little is known of his thoughts or character from his own hand. As Bouquet observed, "I believe Colonel Montgomery would rather fight two battles than write a single letter." The National Museums of Scotland

Sardinian army and with the Swiss guards in Holland, and was an excellent complement to Forbes. The relationship between these two men (who because of different nationalities corresponded in French), was critical to the campaign because General Forbes was a dying man. It is not known for certain what disease afflicted the General, which he described as "a Cursed flux." The illness, coupled with the rigors of travel, caused him acute pain and deprivation of strength, and sometimes made him as "weak as a new born infant." He would be compelled to depend without question on Bouquet's judgment at the front. In effect, Forbes became the planner and Bouquet the executor.

In spring, 1758, while in Philadelphia, Forbes began to develop his plan of operations. His forces would consist of the 1,300-man First Highland battalion; several companies of the Royal American Regiment (Sixtieth Foot); the three-battalion Pennsylvania Regiment; two Virginia regiments; three detachments from Maryland, Delaware and North Carolina; and forty Royal Artillerists. The promised Cherokee and Catawba warriors also eventually joined the expedition, but they would melt away as the campaign slowly ground on. Even without them, Forbes would have an army double the size of Braddock's command.

Forbes favored the European strategy of Lancelot, Comte Turpin de Crissé, who in his *Essai sur l'Art de la Guerre* (Essay on the Art of War), 1754, called for a "protected advance." A deliberate, methodical march through enemy country was required, consolidating advances by building posts and supply bases at appropriate intervals. The Scottish General decided to avoid Braddock's errors by constructing substantial forts every forty miles or so from Carlisle to Fort Cumberland and then by proceeding along the old Braddock Road. Forbes hoped to take advantage of resources available from the granary of southeastern Pennsylvania. Acting upon counsel available from engineers and officers, and following a constant stream of letters, Forbes reversed himself. He now would bypass the Braddock Road altogether and drive west across Pennsylvania from Raystown to the Forks of the Ohio. Although it was a new route (following the Raystown Indian Path) over a most rugged terrain, the hundred-mile "Forbes Road" could save forty miles, avoid several rivers and provide forage for the thousands of horses and cattle.

The Virginians, led by Colonel Washington, were flabbergasted by this apparently lunatic plan to ignore

The Long Land Pattern musket, or "King's Arm," popularly known as the "Brown Bess," the weapon of the British infantryman of the period. Private Collection

49

*The Allegheny Mountains
of western Pennsylvania.*

the "beaten path...the best passage through the mountains." Washington spent much time pouting about the change, fuming, "All is lost! All is lost, by heavens! Our enterprise [will be] ruined." The Virginians had economic reasons to be upset, since they believed that whatever road was opened to the Forks would become the commercial highway to the west after the war.

After pushing the road eighty miles from Carlisle to Raystown, Colonel Bouquet, still waiting for his deathly ill commander, faced the mountainous task of training and supplying his growing army. He collected food and equipment for 5,000 along with the hundreds of wagons and horses necessary to haul everything over the mountains. Most of the troops were raw recruits and had never seen a musket. In spite of "sorry" horses, fractious officers, smallpox, rats, desertion, and the American fondness for insubordination, progress continued. "An extreme collection of broken inn-keepers, horse jockeys, and Indian traders," as General Forbes put it, was becoming an army.

By late July, with the Virginians still complaining, 1,200 men attacked the forest on Allegheny Mountain, "impenetrable almost to any humane thing save the Indians." Looming beyond the first ridge were Laurel Hill, "that terrible mountain," and Chestnut Ridge. Veteran quartermaster Sir John St. Clair was on the mountain appealing for help: "The work to be done on this road is immense...send me as many men as you can with digging tools, this is a most diabolical work, and whiskey must be had." General Forbes was now in a litter between horses struggling to catch the army. On September 1 Bouquet directed Pennsylvania Colonel James Burd and military engineer Captain Harry Gordon to begin a fort at Loyalhanna only fifty miles from Fort Duquesne.

The new fort, soon to be named after General Ligonier, was typical of the care that professionals took to protect an armed body. Blessed with an abundance of labor and wood, Burd and Gordon built storehouses enclosed by a stockaded fort. To protect the tent encampments they constructed a low wooden outer retrenchment completely around the fort. This post could thus protect large encampments as well as small garrisons.

In spite of careful planning by General Forbes, the British fell back into their old habits. Due to a blunder by Bouquet, defeat was nearly snatched from the jaws of victory. On September 9 he inexplicably broke both

"Bell" shaped liquor bottle, mid-eighteenth century. J. Craig Nannos Collection

A Treatise of Military Discipline, *the manual for drill and discipline in the British army, was prepared by General Humphrey Bland and first published in 1727. It went through several editions (including the 1753 version shown here) until its replacement by the Duke of Cumberland's new regulations in 1756 and 1757, which modified much of Bland's teachings.* Fort Ligonier Association

his own rules and the directives of his superior by permitting Major James Grant of the First Highland Regiment to lead an 850-man reconnaissance-in-force to the very gates of Fort Duquesne. Grant's hazy objectives seemingly were to assess the strength of the fort and garrison, seize prisoners for intelligence and recover captives, and inhibit Indian forays against Loyalhanna. This armed body was too large to reconnoiter effectively, but was also too small to give battle against a strong, self-confident force on its fortified home ground. On a hill above Fort Duquesne, in the early hours of September 14, Grant's command, divided up and deployed sporadically, became surrounded by 800 French and Indians, and "fear got the better of every other passion." This wild scheme resulted in at least 300 casualties, and with Grant a French prisoner, the remnant of his routed force fell back to Loyalhanna. A chastened Bouquet had little to say about his role in this strange affair. A shocked Forbes reprimanded his deputy for nearly throwing away the efforts of many months. Grant had performed no better than Braddock. But with the defenses on the road holding and morale apparently unimpaired, Forbes could at least be satisfied that the theory of the "protected advance" had now been validated—regrettably, in blood—and the campaign saved.

The French were having their share of problems in the midst of success. Worried about the pace of the enemy advance, the new commander at Fort Duquesne, Francois-Marie le Marchand, Sieur de Ligneris, had observed his manpower and supplies being drained to emergencies in the north that threatened his primary

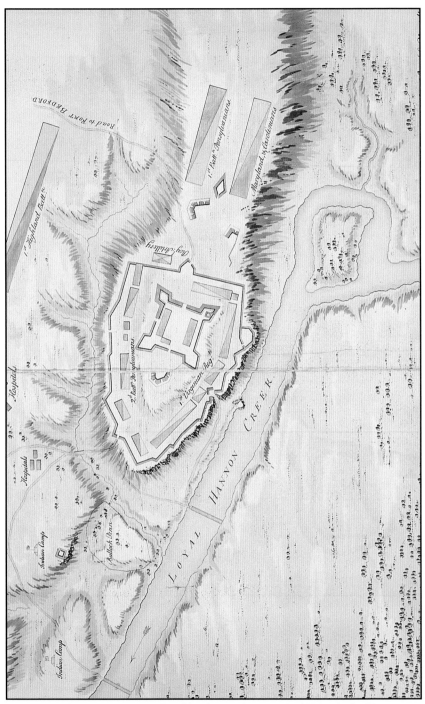

Plan of the Retrench'd Camp at Fort Ligonier, *1758 by J.C. Pleydell. Cumberland Papers (858). Windsor Castle, Royal Library. © 1992 Her Majesty Queen Elizabeth II*

lifeline. Most vexing was the loss of Fort Frontenac (modern Kingston, Ontario, Canada), seized by Lieutenant Colonel John Bradstreet in August, who had put to the torch a great supply of stores and material. As a result, the forts on the Ohio would now be short of food, supplies and trade goods. The tenuous secondary route, via the Ohio River to the Illinois Country and distant Louisiana, was an impractical alternative. Most of the Great Lakes warriors at the Forks, satisfied that they had saved Fort Duquesne once again for another year and glutted with the spoils from Grant's Hill, went home. Should the remaining Ohio warriors be removed from the order of battle, Fort Duquesne was doomed since its defenses were "not worth a straw." Would the British learn of this fatal weakness or decide to winter just fifty miles to the east at Loyalhanna?

While he still had the modicum of a force to throw against the enemy, Marchand de Ligneris decided on a last-recourse offensive raid, with the goal of delaying the British advance until the next spring. On October 12, 440 French and 150 Indians under Captain Charles Philippe Aubry suddenly appeared at Loyalhanna. Bouquet was leading a reconnaissance mission on Laurel Hill, so command at Loyalhanna fell upon Colonel Burd. In a three-hour engagement, large Anglo-American parties sent out to engage the French were handled roughly and compelled to retire to the fixed defenses. Most of Burd's horses were driven off, and he reported a casualty list of twelve killed, eighteen wounded and thirty-one missing. Aubry admitted losses of just two killed and seven wounded. The British were fortunate to get off so lightly, with only the field pieces, howitzers and mortars under Gordon's direction holding the foe at bay. Forbes and Bouquet were both chagrined that their large force had been bested by a smaller one, with the latter complaining, "this enterprise, which should have cost the enemy dearly, shows a great contempt for us."

Simultaneous with the Forbes Campaign were the renewed exertions in the area of Indian diplomacy. Quaker Israel Pemberton, Junior, headed the Friendly Association for Regaining and Preserving Peace with the Indians by Pacific Measures. During the summer he had initiated contact with the disaffected Ohio tribes to attempt separating them from French interests. "I am convinced," Forbes noted approvingly to Pemberton, "that no person understands [native diplomacy] better or [is] more Zealous to bring them to a speedy and happy conclusion than you are."

Royal Artillery in the Low Countries *by David Morier, 1748. Detail of an officer. To be distinctive from the redcoated infantry, British artillery personnel wore dark blue regimental coats faced with red. Her Majesty Queen Elizabeth II*

This silver peace medal is believed to be the first fashioned in the British colonies – Pennsylvania – specifically for the Indians. It was bestowed by the Friendly Association for Regaining and Preserving Peace with the Indians by Pacific Measures, a Quaker-dominated organization that helped bring about the decisive Treaty of Easton in 1758. Obverse is the bust of King George II with the legend **Georgius II Dei Gratia** *(George II By the Grace of God). Reverse is the date* **1757** *and a seated Quaker and Indian preparing to smoke the calumet (peace pipe) over the council fire, and to the right is the "Tree of Peace." Included is the legend* **Let Us Look To The Most High Who Blessed Our Fathers With Peace.** *Trade medals were furnished to friendly Indians by the French, British and provincial governments to ensure good will and fidelity, and as an emblem of alliance. The French and British versions usually featured busts of their respective monarchs. The American Numismatic Society*

As a follow-up, and at great risk to his personal safety, the Moravian missionary Christian Frederic Post carried official messages of peace and friendship, in the form of wampum strings and belts, from Pennsylvania Governor William Denny and Forbes to the western nations. In the process he also gained valuable intelligence about French strength in the Ohio region. Pemberton's and Post's labors paid off handsomely with the negotiation of a grand treaty at Easton, Pennsylvania from October 8-26, 1758. In a great council, thirteen Indian nations were represented on the one hand, and on the other the governors of Pennsylvania and New Jersey, George Croghan and the members of the Friendly Association. The implausible result of the Treaty of Easton was permanent detachment of the Ohio Indians from the French alliance. According to Bouquet it was "the blow which has knocked the French in the head." What Washington, Braddock, Armstrong and Grant had failed to achieve on the battlefield was now partially secured through peaceful means.

The question of an advance on Fort Duquesne still remained. With stoic determination, General Forbes and his entourage reached Loyalhanna November 2. The weather was deteriorating and there were still fifty miles of road to be built. Nine days later a council of war was convened, which ruled the 1758 campaign was over; the army would wait until spring to finish off Fort Duquesne. Forbes, possibly anticipating death, designated the post at Loyalhanna "Pittsborough" in honor of William Pitt.

The next day, November 12, this council decision was reversed. In an incident at dusk, a recently arrived Washington led some of his troops to reinforce a party under attack. Both Virginia units fired on each other, compelling Washington to ride into the crossfire, pushing aside muskets with his sword, shouting for a ceasefire. It was another miraculous escape from death. A British deserter, discovered serving with the enemy, eagerly provided details about the shrinking French garrison at the Forks. That information, coupled with Gordon's opinion that Loyalhanna might be too weak to be held over the winter, galvanized Forbes into action. A 2,500-man force with artillery trekked over Chestnut Ridge and, meeting no resistance, by November 24 was at Turtle Creek not far from Braddock's old field of battle. A great explosion had been heard, and scouts brought back word that Fort Duquesne was on fire. That evening lighthorsemen were sent off to the fort to investigate.

The Arms of Great Britain. *Bostonian Society/Old State House*

The next day, November 25, 1758, from the heights overlooking the source of the "Beautiful River," Forbes and his men gazed down at the charred, smoldering remains of their long-sought objective. The French had blown up and abandoned Fort Duquesne. Leaving nothing useful behind, they withdrew, some up the Allegheny River and others down the Ohio. The Forks of the Ohio were now British.

The conflict known in North America as the War for Empire (the French and Indian War) was part of a larger struggle fought not only there, but also in Europe, Africa, India, the Caribbean and on the high seas. It was called the Seven Years War (1756-1763) and is sometimes considered a "world war."

The attention of both Britain and France was riveted on Europe, especially with the question of "the balance of power." France, under Louis XV, could not tolerate a stronger country, and Britain would resist any continental power dominating Europe and then turning on the island nation. Since 1714, the British King had also been the Elector (ruler) of Hanover in Germany, which frequently entangled Britain in needless fighting and provided France with a ready target to menace the ancient Anglo-Saxon enemy.

Frederick the Great, King of the rising German state of Prussia, was the military giant who dominated central Europe during the Age of Reason. In 1740 he had seized the province of Silesia from Austria, leaving Empress Maria Theresa burning for revenge. The loathing Czarina Elizabeth of Russia felt for him, combined with Austrian and French ambitions, led to a plan to vanquish Prussia.

The British Crown, fearing that the French might invade Hanover, offered Elizabeth £ 400,000 if she would provide 55,000 men-at-arms to defend it (in comparison with the 1,500 troops sent with Braddock to Pennsylvania the same year). The offer was rejected, so agreement was reached with an isolated Frederick to protect Hanover. All of Europe now mobilized for war. Observing this combination of enemies, Frederick launched a preventive strike against Austria's ally, Saxony, in August 1756. The British sent an army for the defense of Hanover. Its commander,

the Duke of Cumberland, was defeated by the French the next year and was forced to sign the Convention of Kloster-Seven, agreeing to disband his army. Britain's lone ally, Frederick, after defeating the Austrians at Prague—also in 1757—fought a bitter war of survival against the three great powers, with brilliant victories at places like Rossbach and Leuthen, and utter disasters at Hochkirch and Kunersdorf. Even with the temporary loss of his capital, Berlin, Frederick fought on in a protracted struggle of attrition.

In Britain King George II and his Parliamentary allies reluctantly brought William Pitt into the government as Secretary of State and let him run the war. Pitt realized that Britain's small army could have little effect in Europe, and that it made better sense to utilize the unmatched Royal Navy to seize French colonies and decimate foreign trade. This policy proved so profitable that the British were able to provide a subsidy of £ 670,000 to Prussia, while the French government approached bankruptcy. Virtually exhausted, Frederick might have lost but for the death of Czarina Elizabeth in January 1762. That brought a new ruler, Czar Peter III, to the throne. An admirer of Frederick, he immediately withdrew the Russian armies from the war. The war dragged to a wearied halt, ending with several treaties in 1762-1763. Great Britain was left as the major colonial power with a burgeoning empire, and Prussia, the core state of modern Germany, was recognized as a continental power. A humbled France would bide its time, looking for an opportunity to cause problems with Britain's American holdings. That occasion would present itself in 1776.

Frederick the Great at the Battle of Prague, May 6, 1757. National Army Museum, London

*"I hope we shall be no more disturbed, for
if we have another action, we shall hardly
be able to carry our wounded."*
        Colonel Henry Bouquet, 1763

Part 6

Colonel Bouquet on the March: Fort Pitt and Bushy Run, 1763

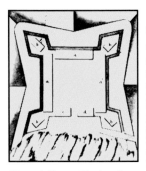

Mercer's Fort at Pittsburgh, December 1758, which was built 400 yards from Fort Duquesne. It was a temporary post designed to guard the strategic point until Fort Pitt was built. British Library

General Forbes stayed a week at the Forks of the Ohio. After a day of thanksgiving, parties of men were detailed to bury the bones of Braddock's and Grant's commands on their respective fields of battle. The General reported to Secretary Pitt in London that he had "used the freedom of giving your name [Pittsburgh] to Fort Duquesne." He also renamed the Loyalhanna (Pittsborough) complex "Fort Ligonier" in honor of his commander in chief, and Raystown "Fort Bedford" after the Duke of Bedford. The Scotsman faced a jolting forty-three day ordeal going back over his road for convalescence in Philadelphia. Suffering to the end, John Forbes died there in March, 1759. Bouquet penned this epitaph: "After God the success of this Expedition is entirely due to the General."

Following the departure of Forbes from Pittsburgh, the rapidly approaching winter obliged the main British force to withdraw back to Fort Ligonier and points east, leaving Colonel Hugh Mercer and 200 provincials to hold the Forks. Logistically, a large force could not be maintained on the Ohio. Winter quarters, provisions and supplies for even this small command would be difficult to obtain. The Colonel worked his men at a galling pace to build a temporary fort. They were well aware of a probable French counterattack down the Allegheny River from Fort Machault (modern Franklin, Pennsylvania) in the spring. Mercer, Bouquet, Forbes and Pitt all saw—as did the French—that the control of the upper Ohio River was a critical facet of the British plan for French defeat in North America. But if this vital area were to be held permanently, a great fortress had to be constructed on the point of land where the Ohio River had its origins. Even with British possession of the Forks of the Ohio, the war for empire in western Pennsylvania was not yet over. It was, however, at an end for George Washington. He had rather disgustedly resigned from his command immediately after the fall of Fort Duquesne and returned to civilian pursuits at Mount Vernon.

In the first half of 1759, fear of a new French assault and visions of being "surrounded by merciless savages" made British occupation of the Forks tenuous. The small garrison of the temporary "Mercer's Fort" at Pittsburgh had good reason to be concerned. In the spring, 700 French with ten pieces of artillery and accompanied by 800 warriors, were only a day from beginning a strike down the Allegheny River against Pittsburgh or Fort Ligonier. It was aborted when word arrived that Fort Niagara was being threatened by the British. Dropping the Ohio offensive for an obligatory defense of this vital installation, the French moved north, only to be mauled by the British and their Iroquois allies on the banks of the Niagara River. With Fort Niagara gone and the lifelines to the west consequently disrupted, all the French forts on the Ohio were evacuated and their garrisons and stores removed to Detroit. With the fall of Quebec in 1759 and Montreal the next year, the war for New France was over by 1760. Fighting would continue for a while in Europe, but the gloomy prediction of the now late General Montcalm concerning Canada was borne out in the Treaty of the Peace of Paris in 1763. New France was ceded to Britain. Spain, which entered the Seven Years War at the eleventh hour as a French ally, received Louisiana.

William Pitt had ordered the building of Fort Pitt, the largest and most elaborate fortress constructed by his nation in North America. His goal was to "maintain his Majesty's subjects in undisputed possession of the Ohio." The plans for this edifice were first carried over the mountains in 1755 by Braddock. Now, with the Forks in British possession, tools, supplies and 128 skilled workers were made available: carpenters, brickmakers, bricklayers, blacksmiths, wheelwrights, masons, miners, limeburners and sawyers. The military engineer was again Harry Gordon, who five years after Braddock's defeat was doggedly at work on this massive project. Fort Duquesne, so formidable for so long because of its inaccessibility and mobile defense, could easily fit onto the parade ground of the five-sided Fort Pitt. After many months of digging, sawing and bricklaying, the almost eighteen-acre complex of walls, ditches and outworks appeared to be unnecessary before it was finished. Where was the European enemy to threaten it? The biggest worry was the annual flooding of the Monongahela River.

As the British took possession of the American interior, one question perplexed policy makers. What was to be done with the Native Americans? All the tribes, courted so avidly by both sides during the war, were suddenly regarded as at best a nuisance and an impediment to settlement. The Great Lakes peoples, who had been allied primarily with the French, were not accustomed to the indifference and arrogance of the British. At such major trading posts as Detroit, Michilimackinac, Niagara and Pitt, they were being denied the powder, lead and alcohol that had contributed to the seal of friendship with the French. Native

General Jeffery Amherst by *Sir Joshua Reynolds, 1765. Amherst's success against the French led to his appointment as commander in chief in North America for the British forces. He misjudged the seriousness of the Indian conflict in 1763, and as a consequence ordered severe measures to be taken against the warring Native Americans, including the deliberate introduction of smallpox. Mead Art Museum, Amherst College*

populations continued to suffer from the ravages of smallpox and other European diseases that had spread across the ocean with the first settlers. Further, American settlers had no intention of sharing rights to hunting lands.

By 1763, many Indian leaders began to realize that their culture and way of life were in dire jeopardy. A Delaware "prophet" preached visions of the imminent destruction of the European race. Those Iroquois least friendly to the British—the Seneca—so long secure in their confederation, now began to circulate wampum belts in the west to enlist allies against the probable day of conflict. As tensions escalated concerning what was viewed as a question of survival, the actual flames of war were ignited by an Ottawa war chief, Pontiac. He had convinced other Great Lakes tribes to unite in an attack on Fort Detroit, May 8, 1763. His act of defiance helped ignite the fire of resistance that would soon envelop the frontier.

This native war for independence that North American commander in chief General Amherst deemed as "little of a threat" had now become widespread. Eight British forts fell in the span of a mere two months. Amherst, who had curtailed gift-giving to the Indians as an economy measure, could not accept that mere "savages" might mount such a potent offensive. The news kept getting worse, however, and droves of frightened settlers thronged to the east.

Fort Pitt was suddenly back in the limelight. Swiss-born Captain Simeon Ecuyer of the Royal Americans and his 125-man garrison, fighting the spring floods, were inundated by more than 600 settlers frantically seeking shelter. They were soon followed by a large force of Indians bent on destroying the fort. The siege went on for two months as what were mainly Delaware and Shawnee warriors attacked the fort with fire arrows and tried to intimidate the occupants into surrender by shouting at the walls. The Native Americans showed such resolution that Captain Ecuyer decided on a revolutionary tactic. In what may have been one of the first recorded instances of germ warfare, the Captain presented Indian emissaries with hospital blankets and handkerchiefs infested with smallpox. His "gifts" did not stem the attack, but may later have contributed to the decline of native population in the disaffected tribes from disease.

Hearing no news from the isolated posts at Detroit and Pittsburgh, Amherst turned to Henry Bouquet, his most experienced field officer, for assistance.

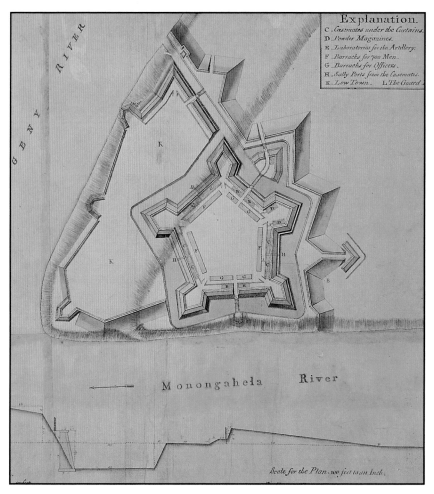

Plan of the New Fort at Pittsburgh, *November 1759. This drawing actually depicts Fort Pitt in its completed state in 1760. British Library*

With nearly 250 miles to cover in little time, General Amherst supplied Colonel Bouquet with elements from three different regiments, the Forty-second and the Seventy-seventh, both Highland units, and a small detachment of Bouquet's own Sixtieth Foot, the Royal Americans. The Scottish battalions had seen fighting in the West Indies, and had been transported from the Caribbean to New York to recuperate from malaria and yellow fever. Under these difficult conditions, on July 18, the Colonel started west from Carlisle with cattle, wagons and a pack train carrying barrels of flour for the starving garrison at Fort Pitt.

After acquiring fourteen "woodsmen" at Fort Bedford, the column marched steadily along the old Forbes Road through deserted countryside, reaching beleaguered Fort Ligonier by August 2. This post had been attacked twice unsuccessfully in June. Bouquet had already dispatched two small reinforcing parties in July, but the fort was still under quasi-siege until his arrival. Nothing had been heard from Fort Pitt for over a month. Bouquet, trying to speed his trip, left the wagon train behind and repacked flour from barrels into bags. Loading these onto 300 pack animals, the Swiss recommenced his march on the Forbes Road, moving toward the abandoned outpost of Bushy Run. This change rerouted his column off the road onto a lesser-known path to Pittsburgh in hope of avoiding a surprise attack by the Indians.

On August 5, after marching seventeen miles in "a vast inhospitable desert," Bouquet's worst fears were realized. At Edge Hill, near Bushy Run, a nearly invisible force of warriors (perhaps as few as ninety-five) materialized from the brush and attacked the advanced guard of the column. By late afternoon, the action had become general, with the army suffering some fifty casualties and a lack of water in the August heat. Using the flour bags he had received just days earlier, the Colonel built an entrenchment for the wounded and awaited his enemy's next move.

Bouquet refused to give in to his fears. He spent the night exhorting his veterans to hold out at all costs. On the morning of the sixth, as the confident warriors moved in for the kill, Bouquet perilously employed an unexpected tactic. Two of his companies feigned panic and "the Barbarians mistaking these motions for a Retreat hurried headlong on...." But at the moment the warriors sensed victory and "thought themselves Masters of the Camp, Major Campbell [and two concealed]

This powderhorn was inscribed in America in 1758 and carried by a soldier of the Forty-second (Royal Highland) Regiment of Foot, possibly by a member of the light company. The shoulder-strap, a product of Native American manufacture, is woven of basswood fibers decorated with colored moose hair embroidery and white trade beads. Horns were readily available to the army from slaughtered cattle, although some of the finest examples featuring elaborate maps were fabricated in Europe. Strong, light and waterproof, powderhorns were especially popular with American provincial troops. The National Museums of Scotland

Companies fell upon [them]. They could not stand the irresistible shock of our men, who rushing in among them, killed many and put the rest to Flight." A quarter of his force was dead or wounded, but four days later, the victorious commander arrived at the Forks of the Ohio, to rescue the Fort Pitt garrison. Expecting to confront an enemy, Bouquet was both surprised and relieved to learn that the Native Americans had broken their siege soon after his weary army had been attacked.

There can be no question of the importance of the desperate battle at Bushy Run in lifting the siege of Fort Pitt. Henry Bouquet was one of the few officers who seemed to understand Native American methods of warfare. The half-moon formation and the "kind of a running fight" tactic were common articles of war for the Woodland Indian, yet many British and American officers would have stayed on defense or panicked under such a devastating attack. Colonel Bouquet, with cunning and luck, was able to change the situation and win the advantage. He understood his enemy and countered him by relying on discipline, firepower, shock action and group formation movement. It should not be forgotten that most of his command consisted of Europeans. Although frontiersmen and militia were useful as auxiliaries, the demands of wilderness combat required well-trained troops and flexible, imaginative leadership.

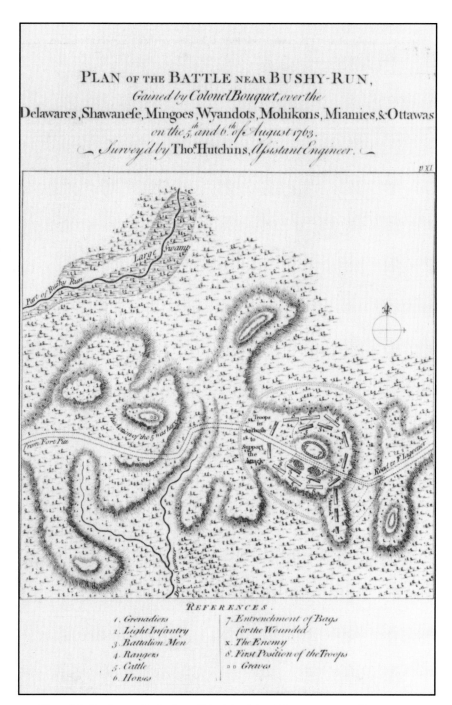

Plan of the Battle near Bushy-Run, Gained by Colonel Bouquet, over the Delawares, Shawanese, Mingoes, Wyandots, Mohikons, Miamies, & Ottawas; on the 5th and 6th of August 1763 *by Engineer Thomas Hutchins. Fort Ligonier Association*

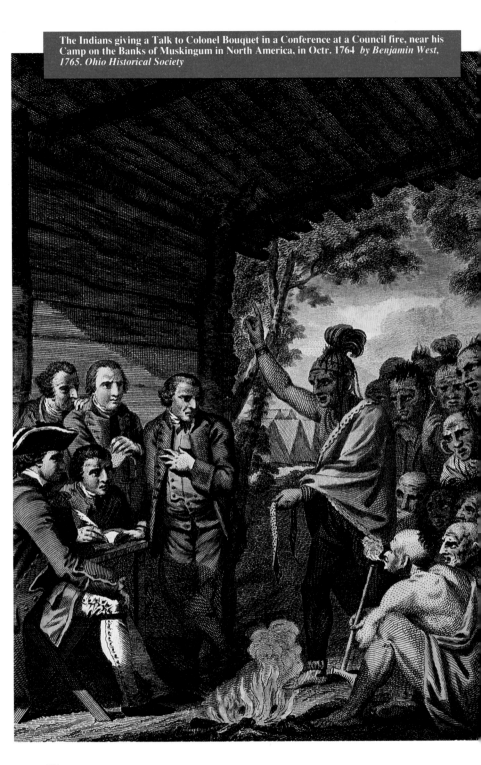

The Indians giving a Talk to Colonel Bouquet in a Conference at a Council fire, near his Camp on the Banks of Muskingum in North America, in Octr. 1764 *by Benjamin West, 1765. Ohio Historical Society*

70

The Indians delivering up the English Captives to Colonel Bouquet near his Camp at the Forks of Muskingum in North America in Novr. 1764 *by Benjamin West, 1765. Ohio Historical Society*

An all-steel pistol for enlisted men of the Second Battalion, Forty-second (or Royal Highland) Regiment of Foot, circa 1760. The National Museums of Scotland

The valor of Bouquet and his men at Bushy Run had saved Fort Pitt, but the war lingered on into 1764. That October it fell to the Swiss officer to lead an overwhelming force into the very heart of the Ohio Country. If necessary, he would defeat the natives in battle, crush all resistance and then dictate the severest of peace terms to them. Based in Carlisle, Bouquet moved a 1,500-man regular and provincial army over the Forbes Road for a third campaign, but this time plunged west after reaching Fort Pitt to "chastise the savages." When he reached the Muskingum River (in modern Ohio) without encountering opposition, the Shawnee and Delaware decided to offer no resistance. Bouquet bluntly declared, "you are in our power, and, if we choose, we can exterminate you from the earth...." Feeling isolated and betrayed, the native leaders were compelled to return all persons of both European and African descent (including offspring born in captivity), and sue for peace. To the Indians, returning adoptees was a great tragedy, the literal giving up of their "flesh and blood." They gave up 206 persons: men, women and children from Pennsylvania and Virginia. Bouquet insisted on taking Indian hostages to ensure peace terms. On the return to Fort Pitt some of the "liberated" Virginians and Pennsylvanians, preferring the native way of life, escaped to the Indians. Later there were a number of emotional reunions of separated settlers' families in Pennsylvania. Another 100 captives were turned over by the Shawnee, some as late as May, 1765.

No one had learned more about this type of grueling, partisan warfare than Bouquet. He offered this hard-earned knowledge in *Expedition Against the Ohio Indians,* 1765. On the frontier, he warned, "victories are not decisive, but defeats are ruinous....all the firmness of the body and mind is put to the severest trial...." In reward for his two successful Indian campaigns, Bouquet was promoted to the rank of brigadier general, a most unusual honor for a foreigner serving in the British army. He was assigned to command at Pensacola, Florida, but died of yellow fever shortly after arrival on September 2, 1765.

Colonel Henry Bouquet *by John Wollaston, circa 1759.*
Historical Society of Pennsylvania

Location was critical to the building of a fort. The French forts guarded the water transportation routes along the Allegheny and Ohio Rivers, protecting their supply lines and preventing enemy incursions. The British forts were spread along the miserable roads over the Allegheny Mountains, providing a safe refuge in case of defeat, and protection for the storehouses of supplies and material.

Another consideration was how strong to make the fort. General Forbes wrote to Bouquet in October, 1758 of his "great surprise" that Fort Ligonier was being built by engineer Harry Gordon "fit to stand a siege," and reminded him to remember "time money and labour and put a stop to all superfluitys." Today at Fort Ligonier one can see where the eastern fort wall of logs and earth, able to resist artillery fire, is suddenly terminated, and the rest of the fort is a mere log palisade. Most other forts were likewise constructed with cheap and simple log walls. Fort Necessity was an example of this form, although about two-thirds of it was covered by shallow earthen trenches to protect troops. The major exception in the region was massive Fort Pitt. Work on this project commenced in 1760, before the war was over. This installation with its large size and thick walls of earth and brick was intended to be so formidable that the French could never again threaten the strategic point of Pittsburgh.

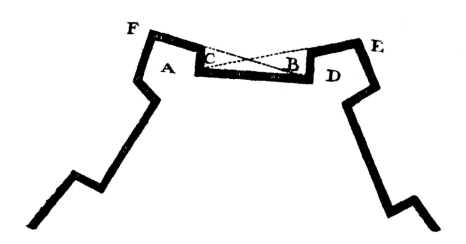

An eighteenth century French drawing of the bastion system.
Fort Ligonier Association

All fortifications had to achieve three objectives: keep the enemy out, allow the defender to shoot back, and protect the defender from attacking fire. In this period a high wall was used to keep out attackers. It was not only a formidable obstacle to climb, but also slowed an enemy force at close range so that the defenders' weapons could inflict heavy casualties. The wall was sometimes supplemented by additional obstacles: sharpened stakes called "fraises" to prevent scaling, outer palisades and deep ditches.

The defenders were able to fire out from musket loopholes, step-up banquettes to enable troops to shoot over walls, and artillery embrasures (openings) and raised platforms. The design of the fort itself, the "trace," also helped improve defensive firepower. The "bastion trace" originated in the need to expose all of the outer walls to the fire of the defenders, which left the attackers uncovered and vulnerable. Each fort wall was fashioned to act as a self-defending unit through the use of flanking fire, with the bastion at each end supporting the other and the curtain wall in between. The bastioned fort design was so highly regarded that only the smallest stockades did without it.

In most forts only the powder magazine, which stored ammunition, had overhead protection from incoming fire—solid shot from cannon and exploding shells from mortars and howitzers. The troops in the other parts of the fort simply sheltered behind the wall or parapet they shot over. The thick logs of the palisade wall would stop a musket ball (although one might pass through the space between the logs), and a ten-foot-thick wall of earth could resist shot of the small field pieces that most armies brought with them.

These forts were lethal geometrical puzzles that no one would dare attack without first breaking down some part of them. Native Americans lacked the technical means to assault forts and rarely did so in a determined manner. The high casualties involved in a "storm" were unacceptable to them. European armies had the training, organization, tradition and technical means to do so. Artillery would bombard the fort from a distance, and if necessary cannon could be moved through carefully planned zig-zag trenches to the edge of the ditch to fire point-blank at the fort wall to open a breach for an infantry assault. When Forbes arrived at Fort Duquesne in 1758 with overwhelming numbers and a train of artillery, he found the French had burned the fort and fled rather than stand a hopeless siege.

"In an American campaign, everything is terrible; the face of the country, the climate, the enemy."
            General Henry Bouquet, 1765

Part 7

The Legacy of the
War for Empire

Bouquet himself was dead before the British colonies took up arms against the empire in 1775, but many of his comrades went on to become leaders in the American Revolution. The ten-year war for empire in western Pennsylvania was a proving ground for the officers who commanded Continental troops at Valley Forge, Saratoga and Yorktown. Horatio Gates, Charles Lee, Daniel Morgan and even frontiersman Daniel Boone took vivid memories of Braddock's ordeal with them into future struggles. From the British side Thomas Gage would help precipitate the War for Independence by his actions in Boston, and James Grant would command a British brigade at Brooklyn, Brandywine and Germantown. George Washington of course is by far the most consequential figure to have come out of the experiences of the war for empire. It was his participation in that conflict, so often punctuated by defeat and frustration, that helped mature him into the man who would lead and personify the cause of the American Revolution and then become the new republic's first president.

The ultimate victim of the war for empire was the Native American. The proud woodland culture was doomed to extinction, despised by its conquerors. Remnants of once great tribes like the Conestoga were exterminated by bigoted "Indian haters." Benjamin Franklin was grieved to hear "that our frontier people are yet greater barbarians than the Indians, and continue to murder them in time of peace." By the eve of the War for Independence, an Ohio Valley Indian lamented, "there runs not a drop of my blood in the veins of any living creature...who is there to mourn....not one!" The same tragic story would continue across the continent for another hundred years.

A great city eventually rose from the ashes of Fort Duquesne. At first, the "woods without end" fell to Scots-Irish farmers and then, later, loggers who fed a growing American demand for lumber. By 1800, both the Braddock and Forbes Roads were major highways to the west and Pittsburgh was the gateway to a river network that carried thousands to the fertile heartland. Finally, the mineral-rich valley, once so wild and remote, became one of the most industrialized regions in the United States.

Today, little remains of Pittsburgh's beginnings. Within an hour's drive, on roads that would have amazed French and British soldiers alike, there are bits and pieces of a world once so familiar to those who fought the war for empire in western Pennsylvania. To the south, the humble, reconstructed palisade of Fort Necessity stands in the Great Meadows. To the east the log walls of rebuilt Fort Ligonier dominate a bluff on the banks of the Loyalhanna Creek, and a quiet hillside in the forest overlooks the preserved battlefield at Bushy Run. On the point at the Forks, a restored bastion of mighty Fort Pitt juts out from a twentieth century highway and dwarfs the visible trace of Fort Duquesne. Nearby, Colonel Bouquet's blockhouse still stands, a sentinel, a solitary reminder of an era of challenge and opportunity, of bravery and cowardice, of victory and defeat, of times now long past.

All that remains of the original Fort Pitt, the so-called blockhouse, constructed by Colonel Bouquet in 1764. It was actually an outlying redoubt, pentagonal in shape and roofed over, giving it a close resemblance to a blockhouse. This structure has survived over more than two centuries of massive change to the surrounding environment and is the oldest documented building in western Pennsylvania. Pennsylvania Historical and Museum Commission

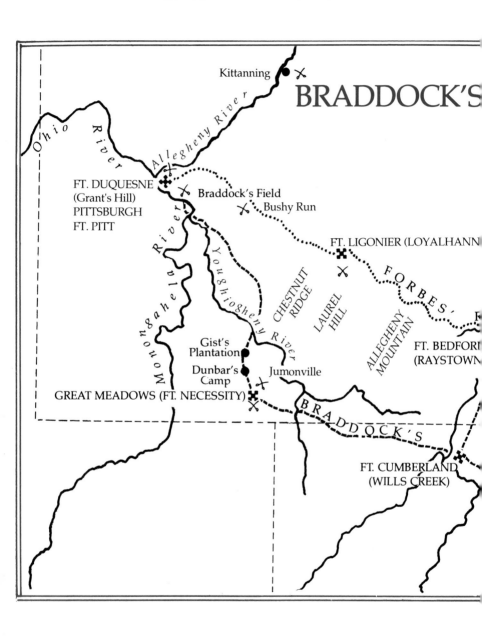

Reprinted from **Guns at the Forks**, by Walter O'Meara, by permission of the University of Pittsburgh Press. Published 1979 by the University of Pittsburgh Press.

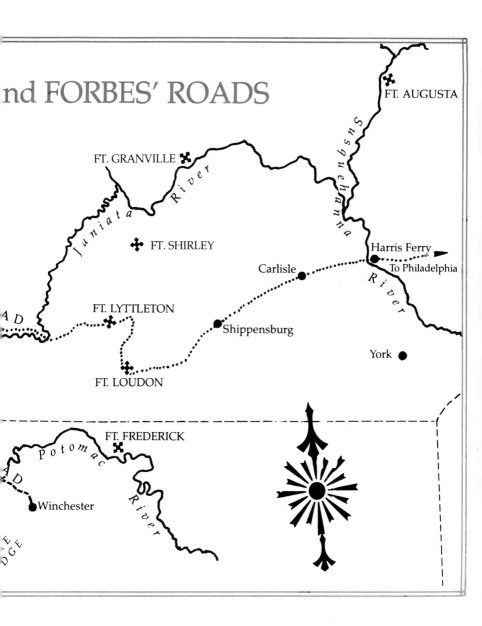

nd FORBES' ROADS

FT. AUGUSTA

FT. GRANVILLE

Juniata River

Susquehanna

FT. SHIRLEY

Carlisle

Harris Ferry

To Philadelphia

FT. LYTTLETON

River

Shippensburg

AD

York

FT. LOUDON

FT. FREDERICK

Potomac

River

AD

Winchester

E
DGE

For Additional Reading

Randolph C. Downes, *Council Fires on the Upper Ohio: A Narrative of Indian Affairs in the Upper Ohio Valley Until 1795.* Pittsburgh: University of Pittsburgh Press, 1969.

Lawrence Henry Gipson, *The British Empire Before the American Revolution.* New York: Alfred A. Knopf, 1958-70.

Wilbur R. Jacobs, *Dispossessing the American Indian.* New York: Scribner's, 1972.

A. P. James and Charles M. Stotz, *Drums in the Forest.* Pittsburgh: Historical Society of Western Pennsylvania, 1958.

Francis Jennings, *Empire of Fortune: Crowns, Colonies & Tribes in the Seven Years War in America.* New York: W. W. Norton & Company, 1988.

Paul E. Kopperman, *Braddock at the Monongahela.* Pittsburgh: University of Pittsburgh Press, 1977.

Douglas Edward Leach, *Arms for Empire: A Military History of the British Colonies in North America, 1607-1763.* New York: Macmillan Press, 1973.

Douglas Edward Leach, *Roots of Conflict: British Armed Forces and Colonial Americans, 1677-1763.* Chapel Hill: University of North Carolina Press, 1986.

Lee McCardell, *Ill-Starred General: Braddock of the Coldstream Guards.* Pittsburgh: University of Pittsburgh Press, 1958.

Walter O'Meara, *Guns at the Forks.* Englewood Cliffs: Prentice Hall, 1965.

Francis Parkman, *Montcalm and Wolfe.* New York: Atheneum, 1984.

Howard N. Peckham, *Pontiac and the Indian Uprising.* Chicago: University of Chicago Press, 1961.

Charles Morse Stotz, *Outposts of the War for Empire.* Pittsburgh: Historical Society of Western Pennsylvania, 1985.

Charles Morse Stotz, *Point of Empire: Conflict at the Forks of the Ohio.* Pittsburgh: Historical Society of Western Pennsylvania, 1970.

Paul A. W. Wallace, *Indians in Pennsylvania.* Harrisburg: Pennsylvania Historical and Museum Commission, 1968.

Appreciation is expressed to all those persons who made the
preparation and production of *War for Empire In Western
Pennsylvania* possible. Special mention is made of William L.
Brown III, staff curator, National Park Service; Harold L.
Myers, historian, Pennsylvania Historical and Museum Commission;
J. Craig Nannos, curator, National Guard Museum and Archives;
and Stephen Wood, keeper, Scottish United Services Museum,
Edinburgh, Scotland. Dean Anthony, Phil Kramer and Keith West
provided additional photography.

War for Empire in Western Pennsylvania

Editor	J. Martin West
Assistant Editor	John F. Giblin
Main Text Contributor	Burton K. Kummerow
Contributor	Bruce J. Egli
Contributor	R. Scott Stephenson
Contributor	Robert J. Trombetta
Concept	Anita D. Blackaby

*To learn more about the historic sites featured in this publication,
please contact:*

Bushy Run Battlefield
P.O. Box 468
Harrison City, PA 15636-0468
(412) 527-5584

Fort Ligonier
216 South Market Street
Ligonier, PA 15658-1206
(412) 238-9701

Fort Necessity National Battlefield
R.D. 2, Box 258
Farmington, PA 15437
(412) 327-5512

Fort Pitt Museum
101 Commonwealth Place
Point State Park
Pittsburgh, PA 15222
(412) 281-9285